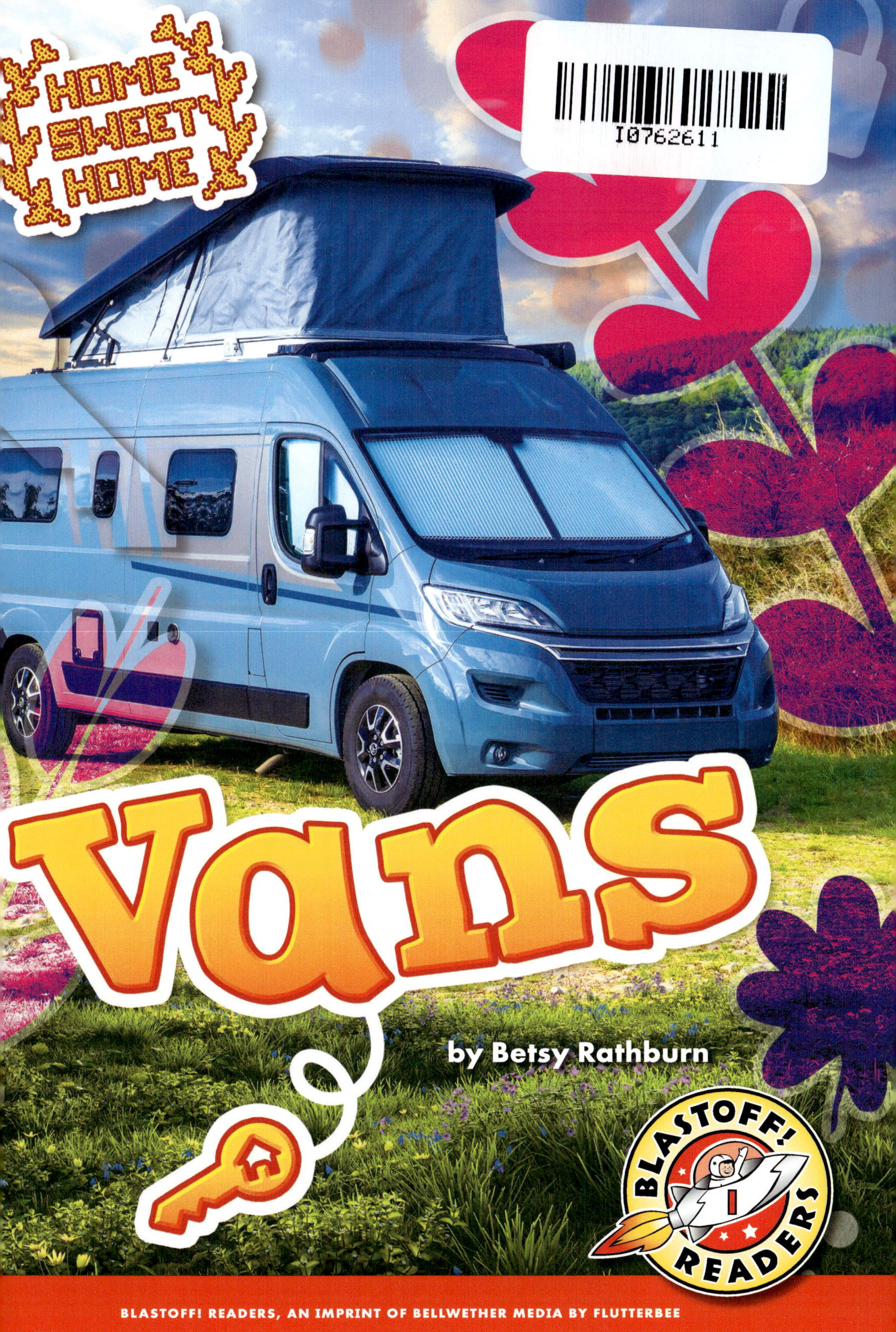
HOME SWEET HOME
I0762611
Vans
by Betsy Rathburn
BLASTOFF! READERS
1
BLASTOFF! READERS, AN IMPRINT OF BELLWETHER MEDIA BY FLUTTERBEE

**Blastoff! Readers** are carefully developed by literacy experts to build reading stamina and move students toward fluency by combining standards-based content with developmentally appropriate text.

**Level 1** provides the most support through repetition of high-frequency words, light text, predictable sentence patterns, and strong visual support.

**Level 2** offers early readers a bit more challenge through varied sentences, increased text load, and text-supportive special features.

**Level 3** advances early-fluent readers toward fluency through increased text load, less reliance on photos, advancing concepts, longer sentences, and more complex special features.

★ **Blastoff! Universe**

Reading Level

Grade K

Grades 1–3

Grade 4

This edition first published in 2027 by Bellwether Media, Inc.



For information regarding permission, write to Bellwether Media, Inc., Attention: Permissions Department, 3500 American Blvd W, Suite 150, Bloomington, MN 55431.

Library of Congress Cataloging-in-Publication Data is available at www.loc.gov or upon request from the publisher.

ISBN: 9798898800314 (hardcover)
ISBN: 9798898802844 (paperback)
ISBN: 9798898801557 (ebook)

Editor: Rebecca Sabelko Designer: Andrea Schneider

Printed in the United States of America, North Mankato, MN.

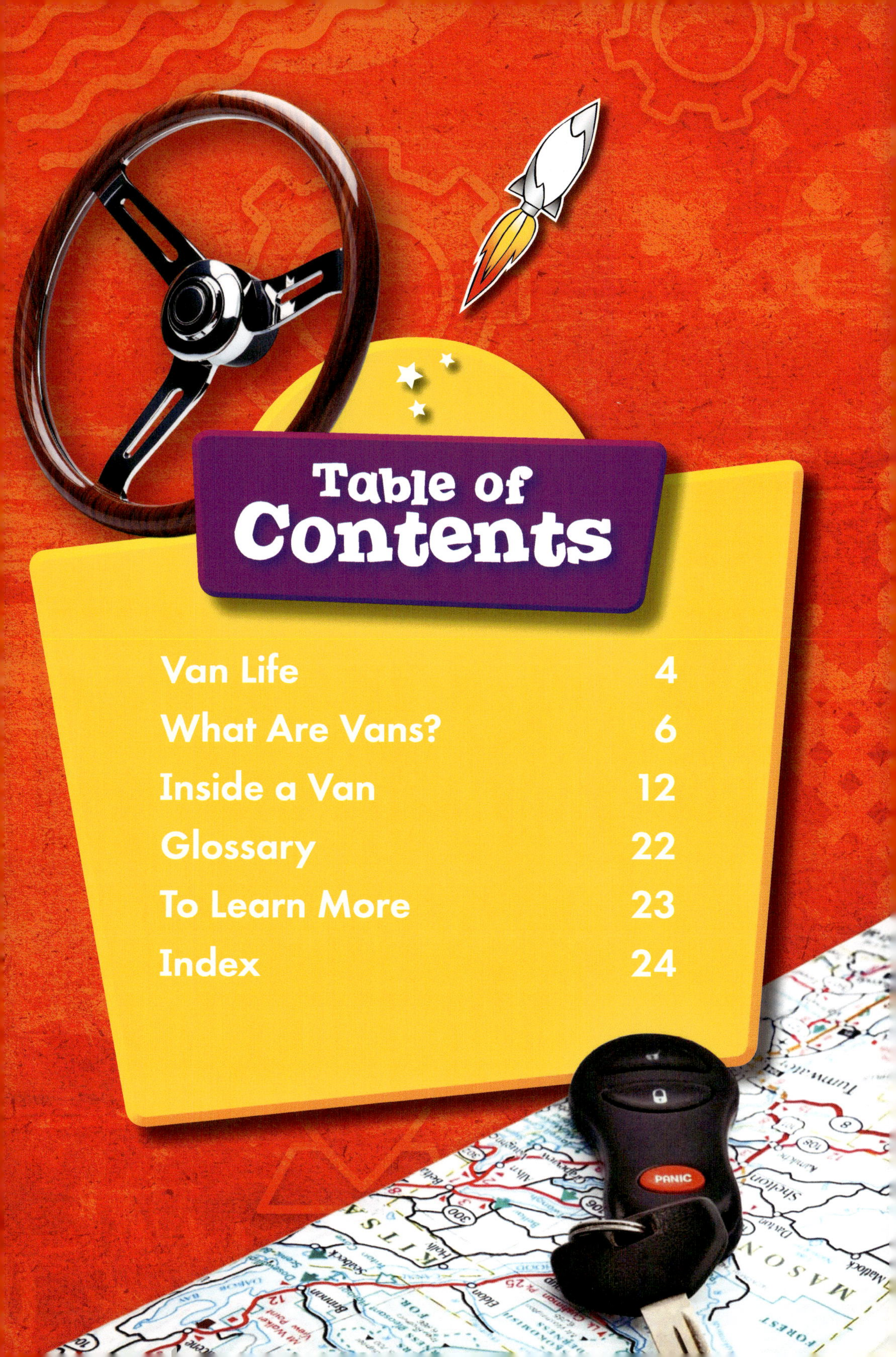


# Table of Contents

## Van Life

We are traveling. Our van is our home. It moves with us!

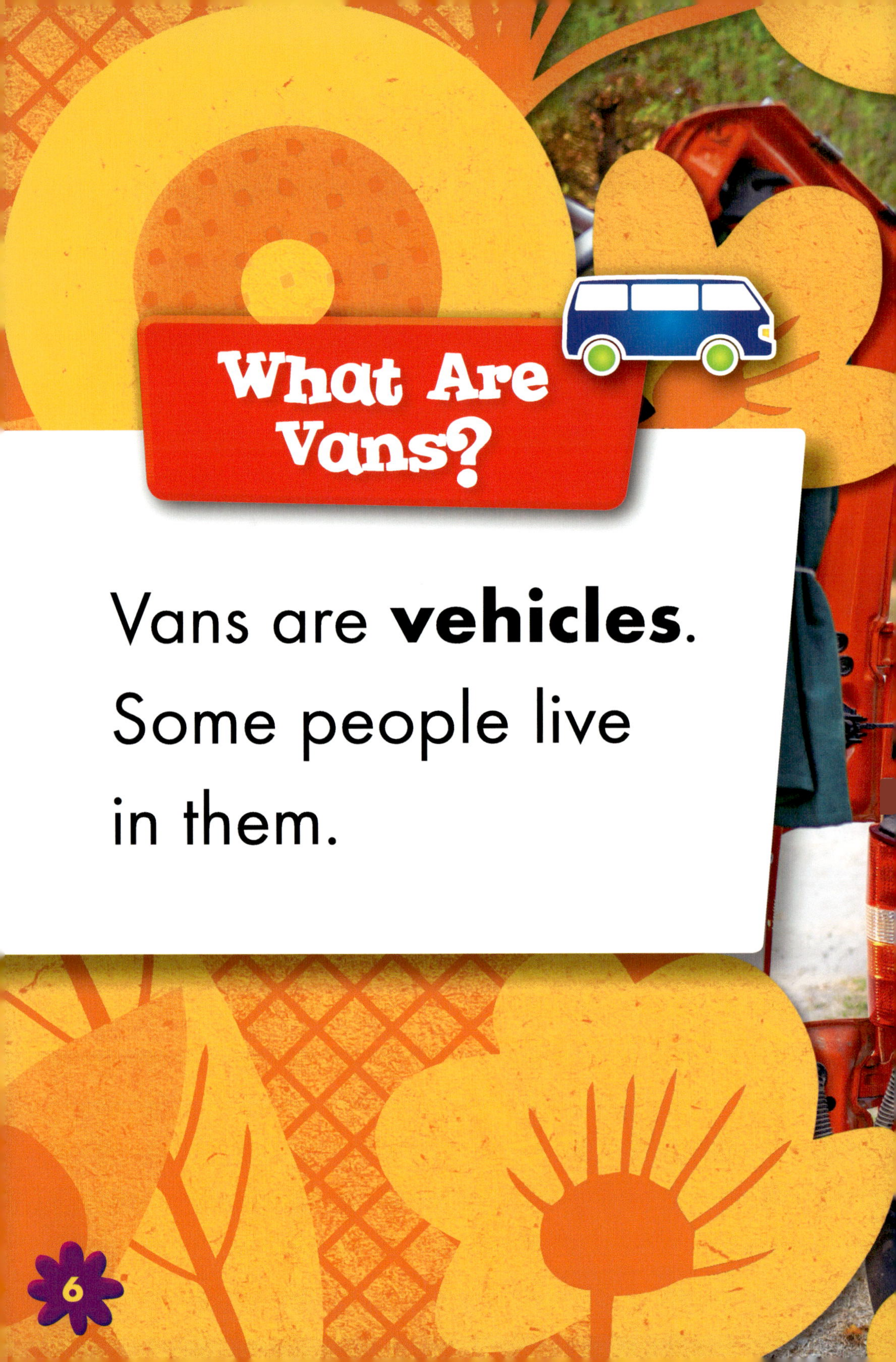

# What Are Vans?

Vans are **vehicles**. Some people live in them.

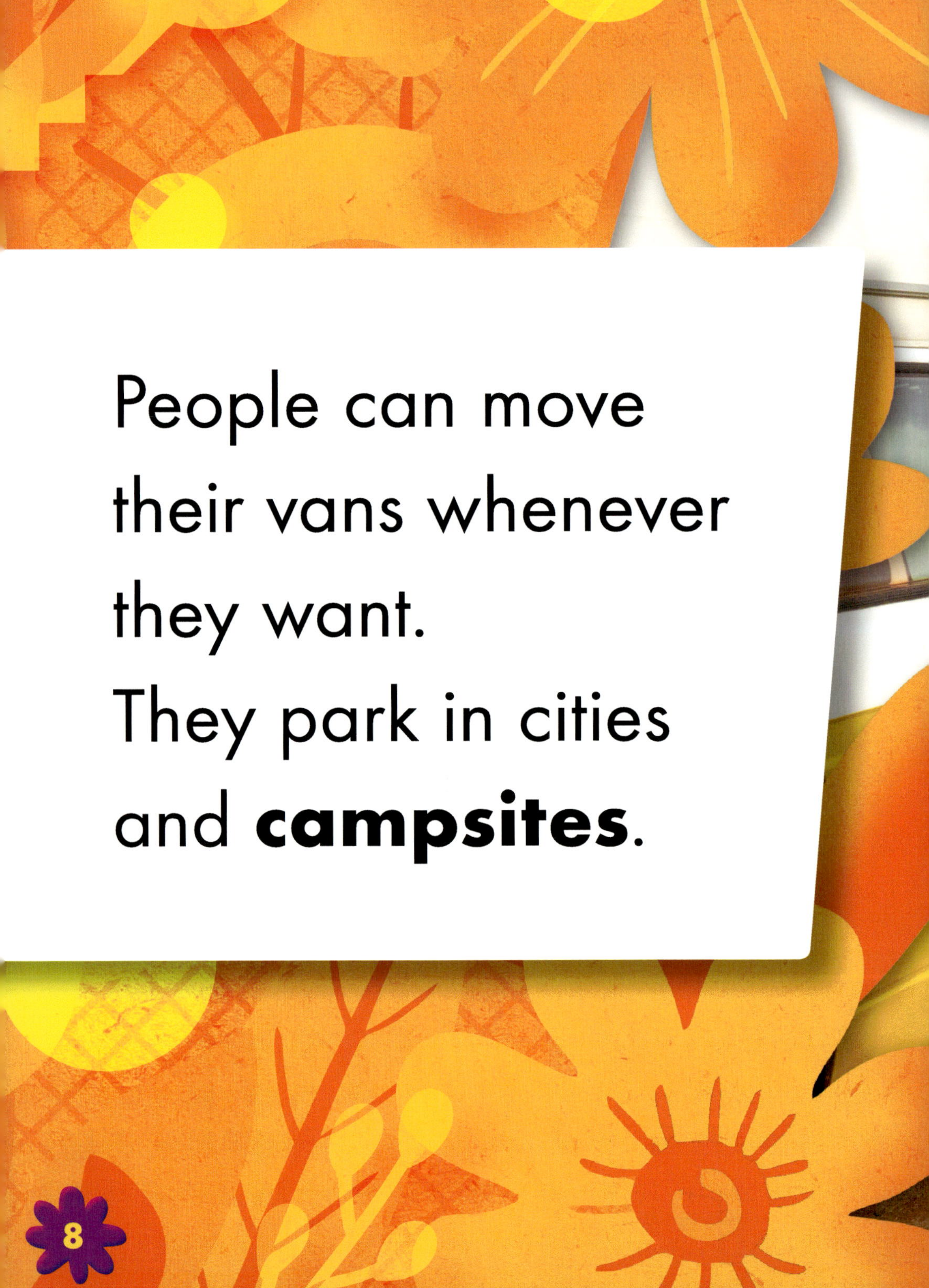

People can move their vans whenever they want.
They park in cities and **campsites**.

campsite

Vans are often small. Some are built for camping or moving things. They are bigger.

Size of a Van
3 cows
1 van

# Inside a Van

The front of a van has a steering wheel. The back has a living space.

steering wheel

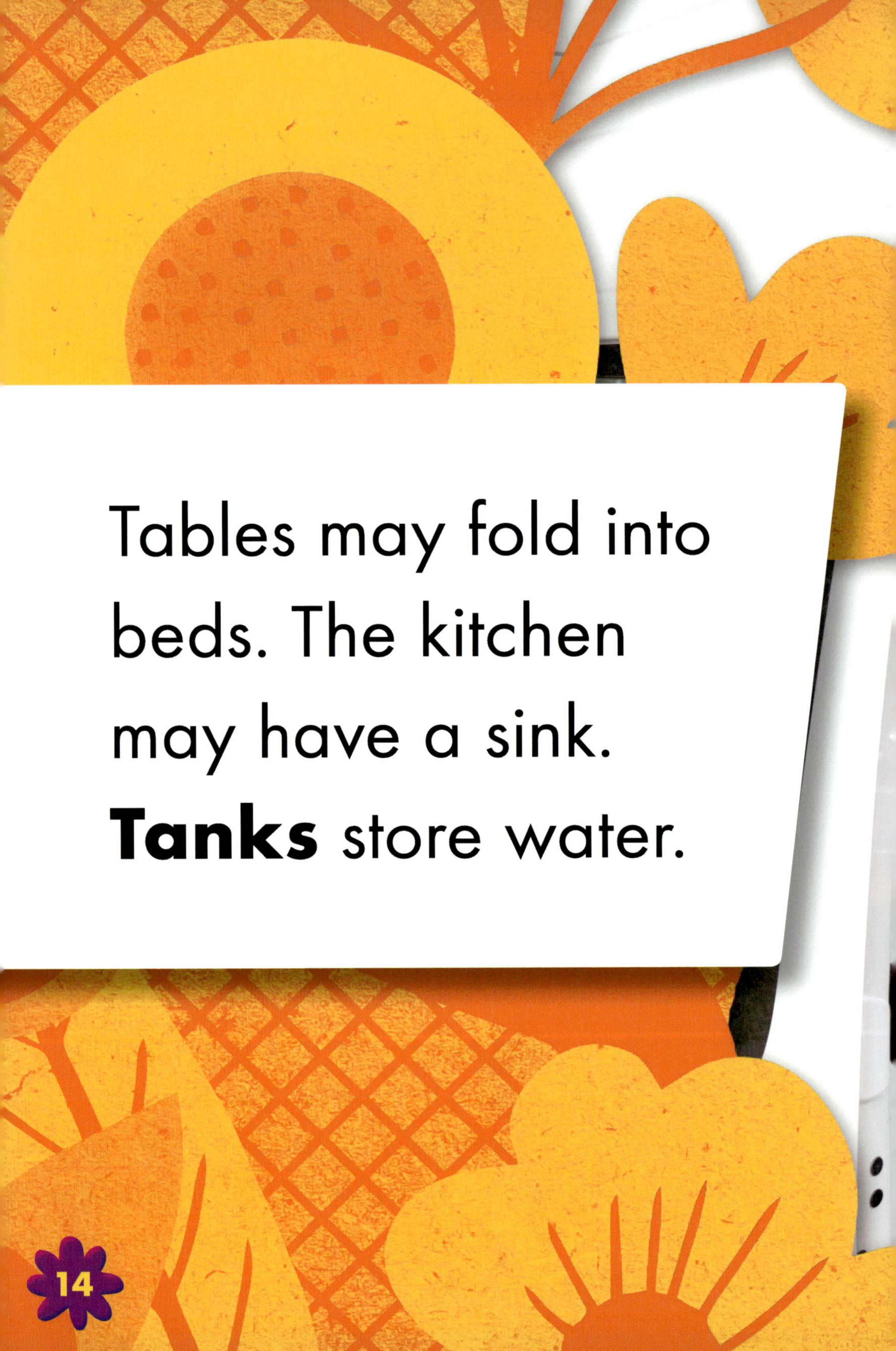

Tables may fold into beds. The kitchen may have a sink. **Tanks** store water.

sink
tank

Small items are stored in **cabinets**. They stay safe while the van is moving.

cabinets
Parts of a Van
solar panels
bed
steering wheel
sink

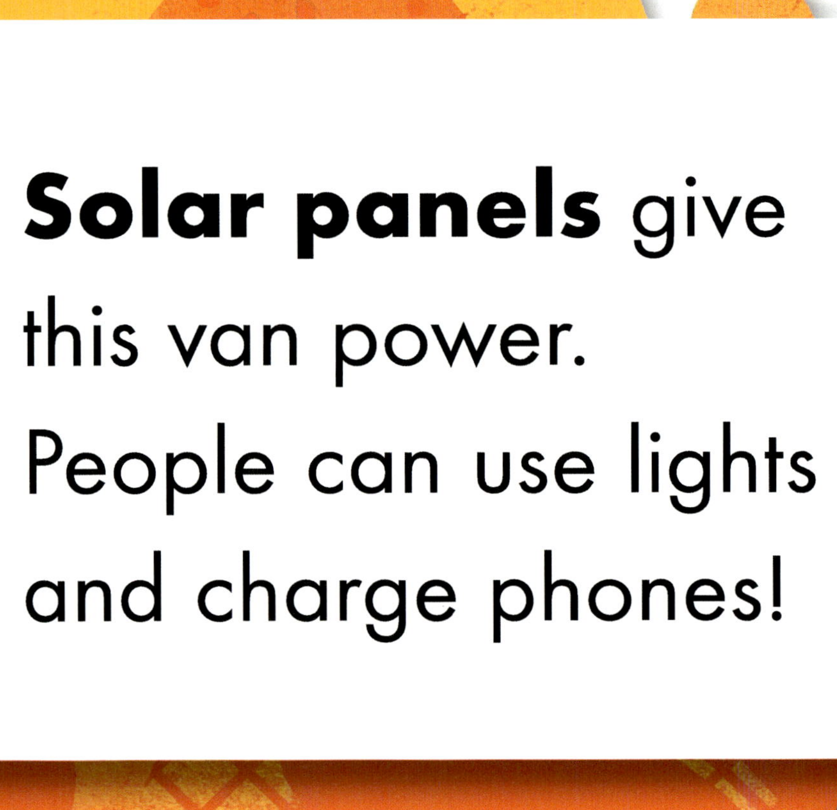

**Solar panels** give this van power. People can use lights and charge phones!

solar panels

At night, people climb into bed. Some vans have bunk beds. These homes keep people moving!

van with bunk beds

# Glossary

**cabinets**

shelves with doors that are used for storing things

**campsites**

places where people can park vans to camp

**solar panels**

items that collect energy from the sun to power things

**tanks**

large objects that hold water

**vehicles**

machines used for carrying or moving people or things

# To Learn More

## AT THE LIBRARY

Lawrence, Ellen. *Homes Around the World*. Minneapolis, Minn.: Ruby Tuesday Books, 2025.

Rathburn, Betsy. *Houseboats*. Minneapolis, Minn.: Bellwether Media, 2027.

Rathburn, Betsy. *Tiny Houses*. Minneapolis, Minn.: Bellwether Media, 2027.

## ON THE WEB

**FACTSURFER**

Factsurfer.com gives you a safe, fun way to find more information.

1. Go to www.factsurfer.com.
2. Enter "vans" into the search box and click 🔍.
3. Select your book cover to see a list of related content.

# Index

The images in this book are reproduced through the courtesy of: Richard Semik, front cover; Lyra, p. 3 (steering wheel); Deo Tree, p. 3 (map); Charlie Blacker, pp. 4-5; karrastock, pp. 6-7; kasto, pp. 8-9; natalie_board, p. 9 (inset); forcdan, pp. 10-11; Jaysi, pp. 12-13; photoschmidt, pp. 14-15, 22 (tanks); photoschmidt, p. 15 (tank); Tomasz Zajada/ Alamy, pp. 16-17; Audio und werbung, p. 17 (parts); David Pereiras, p. 17 (sink); Ibrar, p. 17 (solar panels); swissmediavision, pp. 18-19; Voyager, pp. 20-21, 22 (solar panels); Jure Gasparic, pp. 21 (bunk beds), 22 (campsites); surasak, p. 22 (cabins); Pol Solé, p. 22 (vehicles).